MY MONEY
CHOICES

Published in paperback in 2015 by Wayland

10 9 8 7 6 5 4 3 2 1

Printed in China

Senior editor: Camilla Lloyd
Designer: Paul Cherrill
Digital Colour: Carl Gordon

Dewey Number: 332'.024-dc22
ISBN: 978 0 7502 8919 1

Wayland
An imprint of
Hachette Children's Group
Part of Hodder & Stoughton
Carmelite House
50 Victoria Embankment
London EC4Y 0DZ

An Hachette UK Company

www.hachette.co.uk

www.hachettechildrens.co.uk

MY MONEY
CHOICES

Written by
Claire Llewellyn

Illustrated by
Mike Gordon

WAYLAND

What do you do when
you've got some money?

5

We all spend our money in different ways.

We all make different choices.

I'd like a lolly.

Some people have lots of money to spend. They can buy almost everything they want...

...even if they don't really need it.

If you don't have much money,
you must spend it with care.
First, you buy the things that
are really important.

Then what do you do with
the money that's left?

You could spend it on the latest thing.

No. My old computer works OK, thanks.

You could spend it on something fancy.

You could spend all the money on yourself.

You could spend it on the people you love.

You could save your money for the future...

...to help make your dreams come true.

You could give some of your money away
to people who need it more than you...

...or to things you feel are important.

There are many different things you can do with your money.

But only one person can decide what to do, and that person is YOU!

Notes For Parents and Teachers

We all need to be able to manage our money and make financial decisions. The four books in the 'Your Money' series are intended as a first step along this path. Based on children's everyday lives, the series is a light-hearted introduction to money, everyday financial transactions, planning and saving and financial choices.

'My Money Choices' examines how different people spend their money, according to their different financial circumstances, attitudes and values. It looks at the differences between 'wants' and 'needs' and explores the choices we make when we spend our money, and how these affect other people.

Suggested follow-up activities

• Cut out and price some pictures of things that a child might buy with a one-pound coin — e.g. ice cream (50p), sweets (40p), a bunch of flowers (60p), a toy bracelet (45p) or toy car (50p) — and stick them on a piece of paper. Which one would he or she choose? What would the child buy if he or she had to buy something for a friend, too?

• Cut out some pictures from a magazine of all sorts of things that children want and some of the things they need (e.g. shoes, paper, pencil, bed, cake, banana, fashionable bag or phone, snack, bike, hat, sunglasses etc.). Talk through the differences between wants and needs. Then ask your child to look at the pictures and pick out which is which.

- Imagine you are going to start a new charity. Think about the cause you want to support. Think of a name for your charity. Then draw a poster for it, asking people to help.

- There are many different charities. Which ones have the children heard of? Which ones do they think are the most important? Are they aware of national fundraising days, such as 'Children in Need' or 'Red Nose Day'? What could they do to raise money for them?

- Ask children to think about how they spend their money. Ask them to make a drawing of four different things they like to do with their money, and label them.

- Make a collection of pictures that feature things that are very important in life, things that are quite important and things that are less important. Stick them on a big piece of paper and talk about them with your children. Can they sort them out? Which do they think are the most important?

BOOKS TO READ

'Learning About Money: Saving Money' by Mary Firestone
(First Fact Books, 2004)
'Using Money' by Rebecca Rissman (Heinemann Library, 2010)

USEFUL WEBSITES

www.pfeg.org
www.mymoneyonline.org

INDEX